LITTLE STABLE, LITTLE STABLE ...

BY: JUDY SCHERA

AuthorHouse™`
1663 Liberty Drive
Bloomington, IN 47403
www.authorhouse.com
Phone: 1 (800) 839-8640

Because of the dynamic nature of the Internet, any web addresses or links contained in this book may have changed
since publication and may no longer be valid. The views expressed in this work are solely those of the author and do not
necessarily reflect the views of the publisher, and the publisher hereby disclaims any responsibility for them.

Any people depicted in stock imagery provided by Getty Images are models,
and such images are being used for illustrative purposes only.
Certain stock imagery © Getty Images.

This book is printed on acid-free paper.

ISBN: 978-1-4490-5766-4 (sc)

Library of Congress Control Number: 2009913065

Print information available on the last page.

Published by AuthorHouse 09/05/2019

authorHOUSE®

LITTLE STABLE, LITTLE STABLE

JUDY SCHERA

Dedicated to my Pre-K children at St. Paul's School... you always made my heart sing!

Little stable, little stable...
Tell me what you see tonight.

"I see a big star,
bright and shiny...
high above my roof tonight."

Little stable, little stable...
Tell me what you hear tonight.

"I hear the music of the angels...
dancing on my roof tonight."

Little stable, little stable...
Tell me what you feel tonight.

I feel the love of Little Jesus...
Born beneath my roof tonight!"

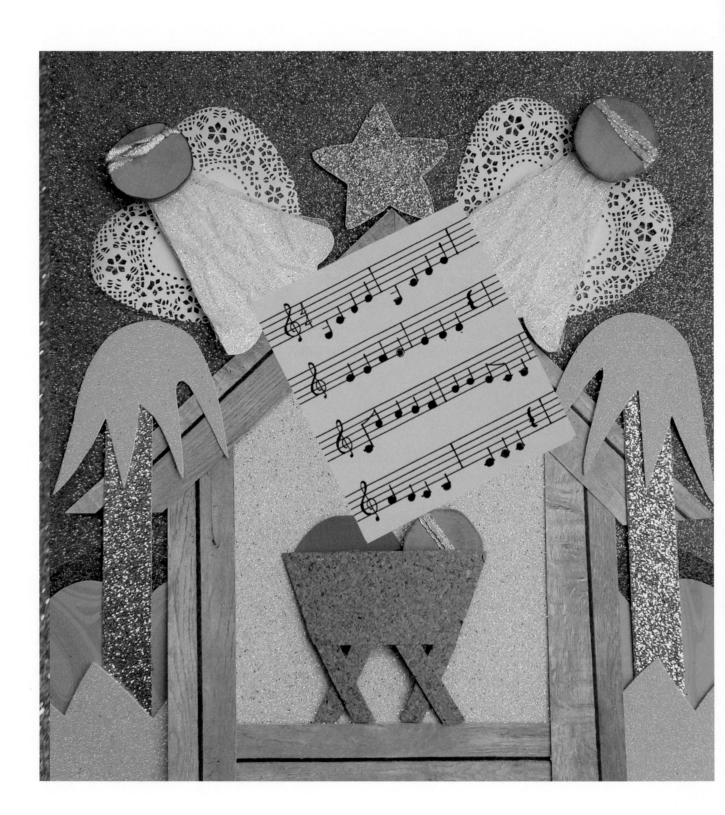

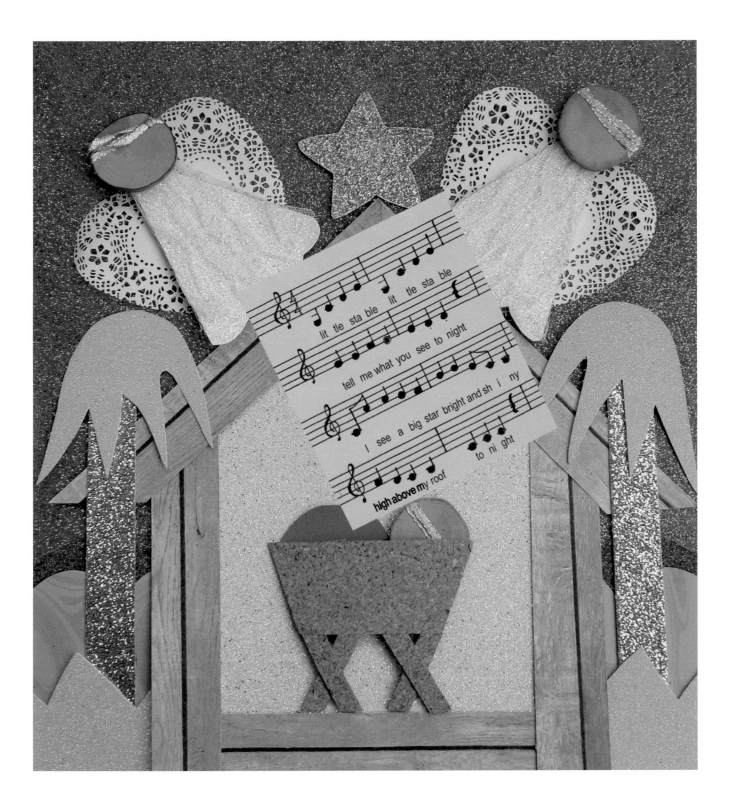

Judy Schera has been bringing the faith to young children through art and music for the past 30 years.

Printed in the United States
By Bookmasters